COMMON SENSE

Pro Beneficcium Omnis

COMMON SENSE;

ADDRESSED TO THE

INHABITANTS

of

AMERICA

John Lollar

The Author may be contacted through his publicist at:

SOterik Publishing, LLC
981 Highway 98 East, Suite 3420
Destin, Florida 32541-2525
(850) 301-0223
soterik@live.com

Library of Congress Catologing-in-Publication Data is available upon request.

ISBN-10: 146-1122-171
ISBN-13: 978-1461122173

For my wife, Nicci

And for my children,
Stephanie and John II

But most especially for
my younger daughter, Katy,
who I believe will shake the
pillars of the world

CONTENTS

COMMON SENSE;

ADDRESSED TO THE

INHABITANTS

of

AMERICA

Introduction

"PERHAPS the sentiments contained in the following pages, are not yet sufficiently fashionable to procure them general favor; a long habit of not thinking a thing wrong, gives it a superficial appearance of being right, and raises at first a formidable outcry in defense of custom. But tumult soon subsides. Time makes more converts than reason.

As a long and violent abuse of power is generally the means of calling the right of it in question, (and in matters too which might never have been thought of, had not the sufferers been aggravated into the inquiry,) and as the king of England hath undertaken in his own right, to support the parliament in what he calls theirs, and as the good people of this country are grievously oppressed by the combination, they have an undoubted privilege to inquire into the pretensions of both, and equally to reject the usurpations of either.

In the following sheets, the author hath studiously avoided every thing which is personal among ourselves. Compliments as well as censure to individuals make no part thereof. The wise and the worthy need not the triumph of a pamphlet; and those whose sentiments are injudicious or unfriendly, will cease of themselves, unless too much pains is bestowed upon their conversion.

The cause of America is, in a great measure, the cause of all mankind. Many circumstances have, and will arise, which are not local, but universal, and through which the principles of all lovers of mankind are affected, and in the event of which, their affections are interested. The laying a country desolate with fire and sword, declaring war against the natural rights of all mankind, and extirpating the defenders thereof from the face of the earth, is the concern of every man to whom nature hath given the power of feeling; of which class, regardless of party censure, is THE AUTHOR."

Thomas Paine wrote those words in Philadelphia in 1776, and those words, and those that followed in the original pamphlet, "Common Sense," helped to spark a revolution that was to change the world.

Paine was no great leader. He was an educated person in a time before mandatory education, which was a definite advantage, but Paine was born and raised in England where he was a stay maker in his father's corset factory. Paine migrated to America in 1774, some say under the stewardship of Benjamin Franklin, and he took an oath making him a citizen of Philadelphia in 1775.

Paine's inspirational pamphlet became a wild sensation in both the American colonies and in Europe, but the author was often derided by critics as being, "A corset maker by trade, a journalist by profession, and a propagandist by inclination."

Paine was just a man. A man that was wise enough to look around and see inequity and injustice, and a man that was brave enough to take a stand against it.

I am not a great man. I am just a man that sees inequity and injustice in our own society, and a man who is willing to take a stand against it.

We are no longer oppressed by a foreign King, but we have allowed a defacto American aristocracy to take the place of the monarchy that Paine helped us to throw off.

We have traded the injustice of rule by those with hereditary titles for the oppression and inequity of suffering under the yoke of those that are the beneficiaries of dynastic fortunes. And we willingly accept being ruled by those of this all but royal class, which we ourselves have created and allowed to perpetuate.

America is once again in need of some common sense, and knowing a bit about Paine, I do not believe that he would mind my borrowing his title, or expanding upon his premise.

It is time for yet another revolution in this country. Not an uprising of blood and guns, but a coup of right and reason, and of ballot and bravery.

I invite you read and to act, and to join me in this intellectual uprising; an insurrection of ideas that can once again remake this nation for We the People, for the better.

THE AUTHOR

"I hold it, that a little rebellion, now and then, is a good thing."

-Thomas Jefferson

"If not now, when? If not us, who?"

-Robert F. Kennedy & Ronald W. Reagan

Of the Origin and Design of Government in general, with concise Remarks on the American Condition.

The Majority of We the People find government and economics to be a bore, and that is exactly how those that controls our government and our economics like it.

The hierarchy that runs this country does everything within its considerable power to make the governmental process, and its attendant economic infrastructure, as confusing and mind-boggling as possible. They do this so that We the People, will simply shake our weary heads in subservient acquiescence and not attempt to interfere with their running of the program.

I recognize the fact that very few people share my fascination and enthusiasm for politics and economics, but a basic understanding of these things are important for you, the reader, to understand just how powerful you, the citizen, are. Those that rule this country do not want you to come to that realization. In fact, the very idea of such a thing will scare the hell out of them.

This little book will be attacked by almost every politician now holding office. They will describe this author as uneducated, unqualified, socialist, communist, fascist, un-American, unholy, left-wing, and just plain stupid. Sometimes they will be right, but more often than not they will simply be panicked.

The modern politician is so much a stranger to the truth that they do not recognize it any longer, and the last thing that they want is an electorate (that's you) that can recognize them for the charlatans that they are.

So please, bear with me for the few pages of this chapter, as I share with you just how we came to be where we are politically in America. I promise to make the reading as informative and as entertaining as possible, without regurgitating too many quotes and dates. And I promise you the truth, even when it is unpleasant.

In truth, the Founding Fathers that formed this imperfect union believed that the origin and design of government, or the purpose of government when stated in more modern terms, is to serve the People; and that the People are you and me; assuming that you, like me, are a white, property owning male.

The Founding Fathers were indeed great and courageous men. They came together and put their lives on the line to make America free, for had the revolution failed they would almost certainly been hunted down and executed by the loyal minions of King George. But a bit too much is made of the altruism of the Founders.

All of the Founders where propertied white males, and the vast majority of them were wealthy men of business and agriculture. The revolution most certainly served to set free all white American men from English oppression, but the Founding Fathers, and others of their socioeconomic status, certainly profited more from that freedom than did the average white male, and the rebellion did little if anything for women, and nothing at all for those of color.

However, even taking into account the fact that the Founding Fathers profited greatly from the revolution, they still made a valiant effort at structuring a government that would be fair and equitable to those that it governed. They strove to devise a government that was put into place to serve the People, and not to be served by them.

To that end the Founders came together after the revolution and wrote our Constitution, which forms the framework on which our government is constructed.

Being the father of growing and grown children, I have occasionally had the opportunity to speak to young people on the subject of government and politics. At such times I almost always begin the discussions by producing a copy of the Constitution, which rarely leaves my side, and another much larger volume. I then ask my young students which of the unidentified books is the Constitution. The youngsters will then examine the two books; one small, unassuming and demure, and the other a cumbersome tome, and then almost invariably select the larger as the Constitution. This, of course, is wrong.

Our Constitution is a marvel of brevity, coming in at only 4,440 words; making it the shortest national Constitution in the world. A copy of the completed work will easily slip into almost any average sized pocket.

The Constitution of the United States clearly and concisely spells out the role of the federal government as it was foreseen by the Founding Fathers. They are:

1. The formation of the federal government.
2. The election process.
3. Forming and passing laws.
4. Levying taxes.
5. Borrowing money.
6. Regulating foreign trade.
7. Overseeing naturalization.
8. Coining money and standardizing weights and measures.
9. Punishing counterfeiters.
10. Establishing a Postal Service.
11. Providing copyright and trademark protection.
12. Establishing Federal Courts.
13. Punishing pirates.
14. Raising an army as needed.
15. Maintaining a navy.
16. Establishing a national capital.

That was it. So far as the Founding Fathers were concerned, that was to be the totality of the intrusion of the federal government into our daily lives. But just to ensure that there were no misunderstandings, the Founders then went on to list an entire section of things that the government cannot do.

Primary among the cannots is a prohibition against the suspension of the right of *Habeas Corpus*, and that no *Bill of Attainder* or *ex post facto* law shall be passed. And that is point where the average American's eyes usually glaze over, and they begin to snore softly.

Americans seem to have a common and innate dislike of the Latin language; and politicians, physicians and attorneys have always used that dislike to their advantage, using Latin like a sort of code language to keep the unwashed out of their business. The only problem is that you and I are the unwashed, and their business is our health, our laws, and our government.

Habeas corpus is the most basic of all human rights. It simply means that any person that is being held under arrest has the right to demand to be brought before a public court, and to be told exactly why they are being held. If the court cannot show just cause for their arrest, then they must be set free.

A *Bill of Attainder* is a law that deprives an American citizen of his property without the due process of law, and an *ex post facto* law is a law that allows an American citizen to be prosecuted and punished today for something that they did yesterday, and that was legal at that time.

If you have made it this far through this reading, congratulate yourself; you now know more about the Constitution of the United States than do ninety percent of your countrymen. Is that not a pity?

Several years after the Constitution was ratified it was decided that perhaps it did not go quite far enough in delineating some of the rights that we enjoy, or the restrictions that were placed upon the federal government, so a *Bill of Rights* was added. They are:

1. Freedom of religion, speech, press and peaceable assembly.
2. The right to keep and bear arms.
3. The right not to have soldiers quartered in a citizen's home during times of peace.
4. Rights against unreasonable searches and seizures.
5. Right against self incrimination.
6. Right to a speedy trial and competent counsel.
7. Right to a trial by jury in civil matters.
8. Neither excessive bail nor cruel or unusual punishment shall be imposed on any citizen.
9. The granting of rights to one citizen shall not be construed as the denying of rights to another.
10. Rights not granted to the Federal government by the Constitution, nor prohibited by it to the States, reside with the States respectively, or with the People.

The addition of the Bill of Rights transformed the United States Constitution from a document that was historically remarkable, to one that is extraordinary.

With the Constitution and its Bill of Rights in hand, an American citizen was, without a doubt, the most freedom enjoying person on Earth. He was also absolutely male, and almost invariably white.

From the onset of the revolution the entire constitutional debate had taken only fifteen years to complete, and had not required the firing of a single shot between the citizens of the disparate States.

Granting those same rights to Blacks and to women would take another one hundred and twenty-nine years, and would require the deaths of millions.

More than six hundred thousand combatants died during the American Civil War. You were likely taught in school that the war was fought over slavery, but it was actually fought over the Tenth Amendment to the Constitution.

Slavery was not outlawed in the United States until the passing of the Thirteenth Amendment in 1865, the last year of the Civil War. The war had begun in 1861, when slavery was still the law of the land.

The North, which wanted to outlaw slavery, could not simply force a law through the

Congress putting an end to the practice, because such a law would have been immediately challenged as being a *Bill of Attainder*, as it would have deprived slave owners of their lawfully obtained property without the due process of law.

The only way to outlaw slavery was by amending the Constitution, and there was no way that the required two-thirds majority of both the House and Senate would vote for such an amendment with the Southern States being represented in Congress. And even if the Northern States had somehow managed to get such an amendment passed, the North knew that the Southern States would have never ratified it.

The only way around the Southern States rights to hold slaves was to force the Southern States into secession, and to then push the issue through Congress while the South was not technically a part of the Union.

Remember the Tenth Amendment? Any right not specifically granted to, or prohibited by the Constitution was given to the individual States or to the People by implication. There is no constitutional prohibition against a State seceding from the Union, so in 1861 a group of Southern States that was fed up with Northern intrusion into their State's Rights did just that; quite legally.

Two facts are incontrovertible; slavery was

utterly and completely wrong, and there would be no United States had the practice not existed. There simply was no available labor pool that could be called upon to do the massive amount of backbreaking work that was required to carve this country from the wilderness in the pre-industrial seventeenth and eighteenth centuries.

But as wrong as slavery was, so was the North's attempt to usurp the legal rights of the Southern States.

Slavery was a terribly inefficient means of procuring labor. Slaves were naturally unhappy with their situation, and they did not work willingly or well. Slaves were also expensive and very costly to feed and to house.

The advent of the steam engine, which was in a constant state of improvement during the whole of the nineteenth century, and the resulting revolution in labor saving farm implements and machines, combined with a growing antislavery sentiment in the South due to the obvious inequity of the slavery system, would have almost certainly brought an end to slavery in the South well before the end of the nineteenth century, without the needless bloodshed caused by Civil War.

The Northern States knew this, but the end of slavery would do nothing about the disputes that the Northern States had with the South over tariffs, and the greed that the Northern States had for the abundant natural resources of the

South.

Many of those that pushed for emancipation for the slaves did so with great trepidation. Even the Great Emancipator, Abraham Lincoln, wanted to ship all of the freed Blacks back to the colony of Liberia in Africa.

The fact that Lincoln did not legally free the slaves by Proclamation until the wars end is ample indication that slavery alone was not the central issue in the conflict. But unfortunately, the North greatly underestimated the vigor with which the South would defend its States Rights, and what many thought would amount to little more than a few skirmishes along state borders, turned into the deadliest period in US history; pitting brother against brother, and father against son.

So what does a dissertation about the Civil War have to do with a discussion of the present political climate in the United States? Nothing; except that it serves to illustrate that history is often subjective, and that not everything that we were taught in school is necessarily the truth.

The truth of a story often depends on the point of view of the teller, and, more often than not, who benefits by the telling.

When it comes to a subjective topic, such as history, truth often depends upon the book that is used to teach it, and the point of view of the person that wrote that book. But it also depends greatly upon what is in the best interest of the people that selected the books that were used to educate We the People, and you can rest assured that the people that did the choosing were not poor.

If history has taught us anything it is that wars are fought for only two reasons; power and religion. Some would argue that money and land should be added to that list, but the want of both money and land are usually simply a byproduct of the desire for ever more power.

War is the single most expensive endeavor in which man has ever undertaken. The cost of putting a man on the moon, or of fighting AIDS or cancer, pales in comparison to what the US has spent on war, and the preparation for war, since this nation was born. And that is without assigning a monetary value to a single human life.

Claim otherwise as they might, nations will not spend such huge sums of cash to defend moral stances, unless, of course, there is a counterbalancing upside in the acquisition of power.

The Civil War was about the power of the Nation over the power of the State; the War of 1812 was over the power of the United States versus the power of England on the high seas, the Spanish American War was over American versus Spanish power and influence in the Caribbean and the Central Pacific, WWI was over Anglo-American power and influence in

Western Europe, WWII was fought over the same thing.

The Cold War, Korea and Viet Nam were about the power of Capitalism over Communism. And the blood of brave and courageous young American soldiers leaches into the arid sands of Iraq and Afghanistan today over the power of Judeo-Christian beliefs versus Islam, and, of course, almighty oil; and anyone that tells you differently is lying.

With the end of the Civil War, Blacks had gained their freedom, but not their rights. The Jim Crow laws in the South would guarantee that supposedly free Blacks would suffer under racial oppression for another hundred years.

Women would also continue to suffer silently and without the right to vote for many years after the war, and both free Blacks and women died by the millions in sweat shops and labor mills; mostly in the North.

Women did not achieve the right to vote in the US until 1920, and the first real freedom did not come to Blacks until the Voting Rights Act of 1965.

No one can say with any degree of certainty exactly how many millions of people have died to secure for Americans the rights that we enjoy today, but the number would be staggering. And yet more than half of us do not even bother to vote, and thereby recognize and validate their sacrifice.

The origin of our government is an amalgam of all the best parts of all of the great governments that have come before it, blended with the blood of patriots and slaves, soldiers and savaged women, brave men and misused children.

We are the issue of Anglo-Saxons and of Greeks and Romans; of Egyptians and Persians, and of Goths and the Visigoths, and of numerous other great civilizations that are long gone due to the overindulgence of their own excesses, or the lack of indulgence for other people of different beliefs and customs.

We are the byproduct of social evolution and religious tolerance, and the notion that no man is greater or lesser than any other due to a happy or unfortunate accident of birth.

We are the beacon of fairness and equity for the world, but we have lost our way. We have allowed a small group of people to rob us of our national birthright, and to horde the future for themselves.

We have been lied to and deceived. We have believed the conjuring tricks of the social elite that we have allowed to exist by our own lack of action, and we have settled for the scraps from their table for so long that we have come to believe that this was the plan from the beginning, when it most definitely was not.

We have become a nation of sheep, being led by unscrupulous shepherds of our own choosing. We have lost our nerve and our will to do our patriotic duty. We have lost sight of what it means to be an American, and we are all in desperate need of a little *Common Sense*.

Of Dynastic Fortunes and
Hereditary Succession

An examination of the evolution of modern sociological, political and economic systems is a study of the conflict between things that are in the best interest of the privileged, with those things that are in the best interest of the common man.

The drafting of the Magna Carta, the American Revolution, the French Revolution, the Bolshevik Revolution in Russia, and the Cultural Revolution in China are but a few examples of people from all over the world rising up and demanding fairness from those that held power over them due to hereditary or dynastic birthright.

The resolution of most of these conflicts came at the cost of a great deal of blood and human suffering, and in some cases, the resolutions themselves were as bad as or worse than the original problem.

Today we are faced again with oppression from dynastic fortunes and hereditary succession, but these evils are now coupled with a new culprit that is even more insidious; the unbridled greed of the Corporate State.

The twentieth century gave birth to a new

player on the world stage; international corporations that know no loyalty and hold no allegiance to anyone but their stockholders. Companies that care nothing about anything but the dividend paid to investors, and that owe nothing to the workers, or to the environment, or to the people that support them via their patronage.

And We the People are the perfect patsy for this new purveyor of misery and deceit, because We have become addicted to the talking heads and the sound-bite. We no longer bother to read newspapers, and it probably would not really matter if we did, because through their advertising revenues and investments, these corporations now can control the news as well.

This new player is powerful enough to tell us what to think, and We the People are dumb enough to listen.

A great deal is made these days about the intent of the Founding Fathers when it comes to such things as socialized medicine, and those at the very top of the income pyramid in America try very hard to make We the People believe that Socialism is a dirty word and a bad thing.

I am not a socialist, any more than you are likely to be a Socialist. Socialism is a form of government whereby the means of production and distribution of wealth is controlled by the government. In other words, in a Socialistic society the wealth of one citizen can be confiscated to pay for the welfare of another citizen; and we are told that is bad. Is it?

If you are an American who was educated in a public school in this country, you have almost certainly been taught from an early age that Socialism is evil. The only problem is that the public school in which you were taught that lesson is a Socialist institution.

The funds that paid for the public school that you attended, and for your public education, were extorted from other people in the form of taxes, and were then used for your benefit. That is Socialism. Are you aghast?

There is more. The police that patrol our streets, the firemen that protect our property, the garbage men that remove our refuse, and many other government managed services and agencies are all Socialist in nature, because they are funded in whole or in part by taxes confiscated from one citizen, and then used for the welfare of another.

It can't be so, you say. America is not a Socialist nation, you demand. But it is true, and it is also true that a degree of Socialism is not a bad thing, and that it is even necessary in a civilized society.

The concept of Socialism as a political dynamic did not exist at the time of the American Revolution, so it was not debated by the Founders. And had such an institution existed at the time, such a means of government would have almost certainly been rejected by the Founders in whole, but embraced in part.

America had just fought a costly war to rid itself of monarchy and unfair taxation, and the Founders had firmly rejected the idea of American royalty. But the Founders considered unfair taxation to be taxes that were taken from the inhabitants of the colonies to be spent on the people of England, or elsewhere in the British Empire; not taxes that were used for improving the infrastructure of the colonies.

So whereas the Founders would have almost certainly rejected the idea of the wholesale confiscation of a citizen's wealth, they clearly recognized a need for equitable taxation for the public good. The only question is: What is equitable taxation?

Is it fair to tax one citizen to a greater degree than another, just because they make more money? The far right-wingers in America would have you believe that higher taxes directed at the wealthy are wrong. But that is because they are the wealthy for the most part.

The wealthy bait the masses into believing that higher taxes on the rich are bad, and that if such taxation is allowed the poor and the middle class will never be able to join them at the top of the socioeconomic pyramid. What a crock.

The ubber-wealthy no more want you and me on their exalted pinnacle than they want to have lice in their underwear; and that is exactly what they consider the middle and lower classes in America to be; nothing more than nasty little blood suckers.

I have spent a substantial portion of my professional career managing businesses for very wealthy people. It has been my pleasure to work closely with a few men that were the originators of their fortune, and it has been my great displeasure to toil under many more that were second and third generation rich. People that have never known want or work, and most of them truly believe that those of us that were not born rich are simply stupid and inferior.

The greatest periods of economic expansion in the lower and middle classes in America have been at those times when the tax rates on the wealthy were the highest. That was during the mid-twentieth century when taxes were at or above seventy-five percent of earned income above two million dollars annually when adjusted for inflation.

America boomed at that time. Middle class incomes skyrocketed, and so did their standard of living. Interstate highways were built and the American education system flourished. Schools, universities and hospitals were constructed. The gross national product was high, unemployment was low; America blossomed economically.

Prosperity and promise was the law of the

land, and then the upper-class wised up. A hayseed Senator from Wisconsin named Joseph McCarthy came to prominence by sniffing out Communists under every toadstool, sponsored by tremendous backing from anonymous wealthy Americans. Words like Socialism and welfare were made to appear disgusting and un-American, although very few Americans really understood what they meant.

The great American snow-job was in full swing, with citizens turning on one another left and right. Innocent people were persecuted for no reason, and with little or no evidence. People were afraid; and in the confusion the wealthy had the tax rate on their fortunes cut to almost nothing, and they shook the finger of Socialist at anyone who dared to notice.

In order to further disguise what the wealthy were up to, the military-industrial complex, which was and is entirely controlled by the wealthy, perpetuated the myth of the Communist threat. These flag waving war mongers further padded the pockets of the super-rich by encouraging terrified Americans to spend billions of dollars on massive nuclear stockpiles; enough un-needed munitions to blow up the world many times over.

"Military-industrial complex," now that has to be a term that was coined by a Commie. Right? No, not hardly. That term was first used by a Republican president of the United States, very near the end of his last term in office. He used it to warn America of the existence of such a coalition, and to be very wary of it. His name was Dwight Eisenhower, and he was also a five-star general in the US Army, and a man that knew more than a little about the topic.

The wealth of our nation, and the blood of untold thousands of our bravest and best young citizens, have been squandered on the myth of the Communist threat, when the dullest of school children can see at a glance that Communism has always been a system of government which was doomed to failure from within. Blood and money that was squandered to turn the simply-rich, into the super-rich.

As a reader you might well assume by now that I am anti-wealth; and nothing could be further from the truth. All of us wish for comfort and security for ourselves and our families, and I am no different. But with great wealth comes great power, and very few who inherit dynastic fortunes have the wisdom and experience that is necessary to wield that power judiciously.

The problem is that many Americans have bought into the lie that has been perpetuated by the possessors of these dynastic fortunes. That they are the best equipped to lead this country. That they are intellectually superior, and that We the People need for them to show us the way.

Families with names like Rockefeller,

Kennedy and Bush, to name but a few. People that have never known the feeling of seeing an item in a window or display case that they would like to have, but cannot afford. But it is these people that we elect to make our laws, and to see to our best interests. Have we lost our minds?

The answers to the major problems that plague this country are simple. All that we need to do is to make it illegal for any individual to pass along more than two-million dollars in cash or in property to any other individual, except a spouse, and tax all personal income above two-million dollars annually at a rate of seventy-five percent.

A husband or wife should be able to pass along their entire estate to a surviving spouse, and a bequest of up to two-million dollars in cash and/or property to as many others as they choose. Upon the death of the surviving spouse that person should also be allowed to pass along as much as two-million dollars in cash and/or property to as many individuals as they choose. The inheritance(s) would be tax free events up to the two or four-million dollar limits.

A person should be allowed to make as many two-million dollar bequests as they choose, so long as no more than one bequest is made to any one beneficiary by any single benefactor, and so long as no stipulations are attached to any bequest.

Under such a plan an entire world of evils would be eradicated with a single blow. Spouses would be able to pass along entire estates to their partner tax free, and be able to see to the needs of as many other beneficiaries as they choose.

Children could inherit as much as four-million dollars in tax and/or property from their parents, ensuring a life of ease for them if the inheritance is properly managed.

Very few people with large estates are going to allow their money to go to the government, so bequests of varying amounts would to be made to people that will then spend or invest that money rather than just sitting on it; thereby creating jobs and opportunities for countless others.

If a surviving child wishes to continue a business that a parent had started that was valued at or above the inheritance limit, it would be necessary for them to acquire financing to purchase the business, and in order to do so they would have to demonstrate a knowledge of and ability to run the business. Obligating the new owner in such a way would almost certainly make them more inclined to treat their employees more fairly and equitably.

Taxing personal income at seventy-five percent above two-million dollars would encourage employers to pay their employees better rather than hoarding money for themselves. It would also cause most employers to pour more profits back into the business rather than taking the profits and having it taxed so heavily. This would create more jobs and opportunities for others.

Wealthy people would also be more inclined to make bequests to the spouses and children of their children individually. As these bequests would have to be unencumbered, meaning that no conditions could be made on how the bequests could be spent, spouses that were tied to cruel or troubled partners by finances would be made independent, and grandchildren would be free to strike off on business ventures of their own, creating more jobs and strengthening the economy even more.

Worthy charitable institutions would find their coffers full. And a byproduct of such a plan would almost certainly be a sales-use tax on those making less than two-million dollars annually rather than an income tax, and as greater amounts of money flowing into the hands of more people would generate more spending, government tax coffers would also be overflowing.

Another byproduct of the plan would be that the inability to pass along personal property valued at more than two-million dollars would give a new standard to the value of property, and also to money.

Once upon a time American money was

backed by gold; for every dollar in circulation, there was a dollars worth of gold on deposit in the Federal Reserve. This was called the Gold Standard, and for many years the value of gold was set by law at thirty-two dollars per ounce. With this time honored system in place, a person knew exactly how much money a dollar was worth.

FDR, who was a member of another super-rich family, the Roosevelts, stupidly took America off of the Gold Standard so that he could print up as much money as he wanted to pay for the Great Depression, which was also caused by the super-rich, and to pay for World War II, which helped to make the super-rich into the ridiculously-rich.

Nixon allowed the Gold Standard to disappear completely while he screwed us at the Watergate, and the price of gold has skyrocketed ever since. Gold, which once sold for thirty-two dollars an ounce, now sells for well over a thousand, and it is still climbing.

An average new American car that sold for four-thousand dollars before the FDR/Nixon fiasco, now sells for almost five times that much. Prices are out of control.

The two-million dollar bequest limit would almost certainly ensure that the day after the passing of such a law, the most expensive single dwelling in America would be valued at two-million dollars. This would have the immediate effect of driving down property values, primarily on the most expensive properties, but on all property costs in general, to a more realistic and reasonable level, making property more affordable for everyone.

Public museums would be filled to overflowing with beautiful art that was simply too valuable to pass along to benefactors in lieu of real property or cash, and which were previously unavailable to the public. This would also cause an upsurge in the demand for contemporary art, and opportunities for new artists.

University endowments would increase tremendously, as would contributions to research hospitals and legitimate think tanks. Everyone would benefit, and men and women who actually had the best interest of average Americans at heart would have a greater incentive to run for public office on a more level playing field, and thereby have an opportunity to speak for us in government.

We should also make it impossible for any person managing or working for a publically traded company to make more than one-million dollars per year, or fifty times the income of the lowest paid employee of the company. It should also be illegal for a person to own stock in a company for which they work outside of an independently administered retirement portfolio such as a 401K.

Limiting the income of people that work for and manage publically traded companies, and removing their stock options and golden parachutes, would do away with their incentive to artificially inflate the value of a company in order to increase the incomes of those at the helm.

In addition, limiting the income of the CEO of a publically traded company to one-million dollars annually, or to fifty times the income of the lowest paid employee of the company, whichever is less, would also do much to ensure that all of the employees of the company are fairly compensated for their work.

Those men and women who manage publically traded companies, and that are convinced that their contribution is worth more than the one-million dollars per year cap on income, would be encouraged to strike out in their own company, creating more jobs for more Americans.

All of these financial benefits would mean a higher standard of living for everyone except those who occupy the top ten percent of the American population, but that control ninety percent of American wealth. Those poor individuals would have their standard of living cut to the point that they can only afford one airplane, and one yacht, and two homes. That is, of course, unless they want to work for more, and then they can still amass as much wealth as their labor and talent allows.

These things can be done. There are solutions to our problems. But we will have to demand that the steps be made, and the super-rich will fight us at every turn.

We Americans are the progeny of revolutionaries. Defiance is in our blood; courage courses our veins. We can do anything that we set our minds and our hearts to doing. All that we need to do is join together, and we can retake our country from those that have stolen it from us.

Thoughts on the Present
State of American Affairs

I love America; I have always loved America. This is the greatest country that has ever existed, and all of us that are fortunate enough to call ourselves Americans should hold our heads high, because we are the envy of the world.

That being said, I have known shame for the first time as an American listening to some of the arguments that have taken place over the healthcare debate.

Technically health care is two words, not a compound word, and that is the way that the right-wingers would have you think of it. They would have you believe that good health is simply a byproduct of good living, or at least, proper living as they see it. They would have you believe that poor health is almost always the result of over-indulgence, or even Devine retribution for improper behavior, as they see it. But it is not possible to have good health without good healthcare, so it is time to modify our lexicon.

Is healthcare a right? No, some say. They claim that because the Founding Fathers included nothing in the Constitution about healthcare, that it cannot possibly be a right.

The Founders also put nothing in the Constitution about nuclear proliferation, and limiting the rights of an American citizen to possess a private nuclear arsenal. Do those that make this inane argument about healthcare also believe that a citizen should be able to have a nuclear missile in their backyard just in case they get mad at someone in the next state? Of course not.

The Founders did not address the healthcare issue for exactly the same reason that they did not address the topic of nuclear proliferation; in the late eighteenth century there was no such thing.

In 1787 bleeding a patient, or studying the shape and consistency of a person's stool, was considered the state of the art in healthcare. Pharmacology was little different from alchemy at the time, and the best of the healthcare that was available could be bartered for a chicken or a pig, and it was every bit as likely to kill a patient as to cure them.

The Founders did not debate issues relating to healthcare, but they did clearly state in the Preamble to the Constitution that one of their main purposes in drafting the document was to provide for the public Welfare, which certainly would have included healthcare had there been such a thing at the time. Additionally, the signers of the Declaration of Independence also clearly stated that they recognized the right of all Americans to enjoy *life*, which one cannot do without good health.

Of course healthcare is a right, and anyone that argues otherwise is a scoundrel and a fool. But should healthcare be free? The answer to that question must be no, because funding is at the heart of our current healthcare system, as it should be, but so are profits, which should not.

No American should ever be denied healthcare for financial reasons, but every American that has the means should pay for access to the healthcare system.

That may seem counterintuitive, but it is not. Not if you look at healthcare as a right, and not as a business, and that is where that nasty Socialism word pops up again.

There is a reason that we do not have private police and fire departments, because the services that they perform are vital, and we cannot take the chance that they might be denied to any citizen.

Had the Founders been able to foresee the current state of affairs regarding healthcare, I believe that they would have seen to it that healthcare was also to be administered by the government, and for the same reason.

Healthcare never should have been allowed to be a for profit business. Being a healthcare professional should have been what many claim that it is today; a calling for people with great compassion and intelligence, and for those that possess an innate need to help others.

There are those that argue that if the financial incentives were removed from healthcare that the system would collapse. Nonsense. Those that feel that way have never stood as a small child and watched helplessly as cancer slowly consume a loved one, or buried a parent or beloved grandparent because of heart disease, or a brother or a sister due to AIDS.

Those are the experiences that motivate people to make great strides in medicine, not money. If anything, money is a detractor from needed research because it may not prove to be sufficiently profitable.

Doctors should be very well paid, but they should not be rolling in money. Nurses should be better paid than they are, and in a properly managed public healthcare system they would be.

Now I am going to write about dollars and cents for just a few lines. I promise to be brief, but please read on and pay attention. This is boring but important.

Americans currently spend about 2.3 trillion dollars annually on healthcare, or about seventy-seven hundred dollars per person. Those are meaningless numbers.

Do you know why car dealers usually only advertise monthly payments, rather than the price of a car? It is because they found out years ago that numbers like twenty thousand dollars were meaningless.

Ninety percent of Americans have never held ten thousand dollars in cash in their hands that was their own. And they likely have never, and will never, have ten thousand dollars in the bank that is unallocated, and that they can spend as they wish.

Large sums of cash are simply unimaginable to most people, but they can understand four hundred dollars per month. They have held four hundred dollars before, and they probably even have four hundred dollars in the bank. So car dealers discovered that Americans really do not care very much about the price of a car, as long as they can afford the monthly payment. The total cost is meaningless.

Most Americans cannot fathom how much money 2.3 trillion dollars is; the amount is mindboggling and beyond comprehension. And those guys in Washington that currently spend twice that amount every year like it that you are confused, and that you do not understand.

The operating budget for the US government is currently about 3.5 trillion dollars per year, or about eleven thousand seven hundred dollars for every man, woman and child. That is nuts.

There are those, and I am one of them, that believe that at least half of that staggering figure is siphoned right off of the top in waste, bureaucracy, and downright theft. But even if that is so, it still means that the government is spending nearly four thousand dollars per person per year on us. That is three hundred and fifty dollars per month per person. Are you getting your money's worth? I'm not.

You should be asking yourself about now why I would want to turn over another 2.3 trillion dollars to the government to spend on healthcare, if they are already stealing and wasting about that much already.

The answer to that question requires discussion on many fronts; first, I expect We the People (that is you and me) to fire every one of the crooked bastards in Washington before we send another dollar from any source to that sinkhole, and replace them with reliable people that will be held accountable.

Next, by making healthcare public it can be made much more affordable, and within the means of everyone.

Solving the healthcare dilemma is not complicated as the politicians would have us believe that it is. Simply by doing away with dynastic fortunes a great deal of money would be contributed to research centers and teaching hospitals, by wealthy people that would be unable to pass along obscene amounts of cash to their heirs.

Secondly, by making healthcare a nonprofit proposition, as it always should have been; healthcare costs would be reduced considerably.

Thirdly, putting a halt to the ridiculous practice of burying or burning viable organs of deceased people, and making those organs available for transplant to those in need, will drastically reduce long-term healthcare costs, and improve the quality and duration of life for millions.

Next, making regular healthcare available to everyone would cause people to address health problems early, when they can be easily and affordably treated, rather than waiting until a condition becomes critical or chronic, and when it takes tens or hundreds of thousands of dollars to treat.

Lastly, every family in America should pay a healthcare tax in the amount of one hundred dollars per person per month, and that money should be used to pay for public healthcare.

Now hold on there, you say. That is only three hundred and sixty billion dollars per year; that is no where near the 2.3 trillion that we spend now. You are so right.

But never use the words *only* and *billion* together in the same sentence; a billion dollars is a huge amount of money. And you do not make a budget by imagining everything that you would like to have and then spending that much, even if you do not have it. That is how this country got to be fourteen trillion dollars in debt; which we are. You make a budget by determining how much money that you have to spend, and then making that work.

And you must also remember that by cutting out the need for profit the costs of healthcare will be reduced considerably, and by administering the system effectively virtually half of the current costs would be eliminated.

You must also bear in mind that by doing away with dynastic fortunes a more realistic value will almost certainly be assigned to money, and with a revitalized and revalued dollar in hand, we likely be able to return to a more reasonable healthcare expenditure, such as the 253 billion that we spent in 1980, when a dollar was still a dollar, and not the almost worthless script that it is today.

That was simple. Affordable healthcare for everyone; and for much less than it is costing us now. But I can already hear the naysayers screaming that it cannot be done. That public healthcare cannot work. That without financial incentives there will be no new drugs, and that without million dollar incomes doctors will not work; and that we cannot possibly cut spending by that much without loosing vital services.

Do you realize what an insult that attitude is to us as Americans? Do you really believe that without the executives and stockholders of giant insurance, healthcare and pharmaceutical companies making huge sums of cash, that the researchers in the lab are going to stop doing their work?

Do you think for an instant that that there are not highly dedicated young men and women in America today, that are willing to submit to the years of arduous study required to become healthcare professionals for good money, but also because they have a burning desire to help and to heal?

It will not be patriotic Americans that will be telling you that this cannot work; it will be greedy executives and their highly paid mouthpieces that will be trying to protect their position in a place where they should have never been allowed.

We are people, not products, and healthcare is a right, not an industry, and we must stop treating it as such.

We can afford high quality healthcare for every single American citizen. What we can no longer afford is to support those that are making huge fortunes off of the pain and suffering of others, while telling us that we are not paying them enough for their services.

You have the vote. You have the power. You do not have to sit idly by and allow corporate greed to rob you of your health and your future.

Wake up! Stand Up! Tell those in Washington that you are now a member of the Not ZZZ party, and that you are awake and watching them.

Refuse to listen to their lies any longer. Vote the scoundrels out of office, and vote in new people that are willing to reform this country. And if they do not act to do so immediately, vote them out as well.

Demand better. Demand accountability. Demand an end to dynastic fortunes. Demand term limits. Demand politicians that are going to stand up for you, and your rights as an American citizen.

You have the vote. You have the power. Fire the damn president if he does not do your bidding. Fire your senator and congressman, and put someone in their place that will make a difference, and not just a change. Change for the sake of change is useless.

You are an American citizen with a vote, and that makes you one of the most powerful people on earth. Stop letting them lie to you. Stop being gullible. Wake up before they steel it all; your future and your children's future. And for what? To stack ever more of your money into their bank accounts; not to purchase things, but to buy the power that procures your vote.

Stop listening to Rush Limbaugh and Rachael Maddow tell you that it is all the other guy's fault. Limbaugh and Maddow, and all the rest of the talking heads on mainstream radio and television, are just a bunch of windup toys for the super-rich corporate executives and political bosses.

None of them is anything more than a modern day Lonesome Rhodes, whose only function, outside of self aggrandizement, is to regurgitate biased vitriol that is fed to them from their well heeled masters. Their only purpose is to keep the fringe elements on both sides at one another's throats, and the moderates in the middle in confusion, while the people on top pick everyone's pocket.

The problem is not the far left or the far right; the problem is you, because you are not doing anything.

Turn off the radio and vote. Turn off the television and vote. Put down the joystick and turn off the computer, and vote.

Stop listening to the nay saying politicians telling you that it cannot be done, and tell them that they will do what you want or you will fire their ass.

Get angry. Get so mad that your hands quake; and then don't grab for a gun, but pull a lever instead, and vote.

Stop settling for the table scraps of the super-rich and demand your full piece of the pie. And when they sneer at you and call you a Socialist, pound your breast proudly and tell them that they are damn right that you are a Socialist; just like Thomas Jefferson and James Madison before you.

On the present ability of America, with some miscellaneous Reflections.

The present ability of America is whatever We the People of America choose for it to be.

Way back in 1961 John Kennedy told the world that America would put a man on the moon by the end of that decade. At the time that he said it Kennedy had no idea how we would accomplish such a thing. We had put our first astronaut into space for a few brief minutes only twenty days before. Our space program was being run by a handful of knowledgeable but inexperienced ex-Nazis, and our rockets blew-up more often than not. But he said it, and we did it.

The indomitable American spirit can accomplish anything that we put our minds and energies towards doing. America is great; America is beautiful.

America is the only nation that has ever existed that could have accomplished global domination at one time if we wished, but we never even tried. At the close of World War II, when we alone possessed the knowledge of how to split the atom, America could have taken over control of the entire planet with only a threat, and without ever firing a shot; but it never crossed our minds to do so.

America has fed and clothed the world.

America is the most benevolent country that has ever existed. And our benevolence has bitten us in the ass for years.

The world does not appreciate American charity, and they resent our prosperity. We are the envy of the world, and whether they will admit it or not, virtually everyone on the planet that was not born into royalty, wishes that they were an American. But their longing has turned into resentment, and often hatred, and many of them wish us ill.

They resent our freedom, and our tolerance, and our prosperity; but mostly they just resent us.

There was a time when we could have closed our borders and adopted a policy of isolationism, but that time has passed. In the world of the Internet and jet travel we can no longer lock ourselves away. But the post 9/11 world is a dangerous place, and the nut-jobs are out to get us.

Solving our domestic troubles is a relatively easy task; dealing with our global problems is much more complicated.

We have become addicted to oil, and we do not have enough domestic resources to feed that monkey. The countries on this planet that do have substantial oil reserves are all run by mad men, religious zealots, or totally corrupt monarchies; and most of them would like to see us falter.

It is a huge problem, made worse by the fact that the wealthiest and most powerful families in this country are heavily invested in seeing to it that our addiction to petroleum continues until the last drop is gone.

What we need is another Kennedy. What we need is a man or woman who is willing to stand up as President and say that we are going to end our dependence on petroleum, and that we are going to do it in eight years.

We need to put our best minds to work to end the ecological stupidity that is killing our environment, and allowing mad men to hold us hostage.

We need to re-declare our national independence, and separate ourselves from those that would do us harm.

We are a good and caring people, and we will never turn our backs on others that are in need. But we should offer our charity freely; not at gun point.

It is also time for us to enforce our time honored policy of separating church and state, and stop the insurgence of religious fervor into our politics that has been happening of late.

The last time that the American people were foolish enough to mix religion and politics, people were hanged as witches and burned at the stake as heretics. In those counties where the practice is honored today women are stoned for adultery, and people are beheaded for being infidels.

We are better than that. We are smarter than that. Religious fundamentalism and ignorance is what crashed those planes into our buildings in Washington and New York, but it was American bravery and courage that guided the one into that field in Pennsylvania.

We must not dishonor those that have died to give us the freedom to worship as we choose, or not as we choose, by allowing religious fundamentalism to corrupt our political system, be that corruption Islamic or Judeo-Christian in nature.

We should embrace one another as brothers and sisters, and we should let the world know that when you harm one of us, you harm us all.

We should tell the world that they are free to practice whatever religion that they wish within the confines their own borders, but that they are not free to import their petty hatred to this great nation, or to molest our citizens when they are abroad.

We should let the world know that any person who is traveling under the protection of a US passport also enjoys the full protection of the US military, and that we will protect our own with deliberate intent and immediate effect.

We should stop being afraid, and be proud to be Americans.

We are the People.

Epistle to Quakers

"Here ends the examination of your testimony; (which I call upon no man to abhor, as ye have done, but only to read and judge of fairly;) to which I subjoin the following remark; "That the setting up and putting down of kings," most certainly mean, the making him a king, who is yet not so, and the making him no king who is already one. And pray what hath this to do in the present case? We neither mean to set up nor to put down, neither to make nor to unmake, but to have nothing to do with them. Wherefore your testimony in whatever light it is viewed serves only to dishonor your judgment, and for many other reasons had better have been let alone than published.

First. Because it tends to the decrease and reproach of religion whatever, and is of the utmost danger to society, to make It a party in political disputes. Secondly. Because it exhibits a body of men, numbers of whom disavow the publishing political testimonies, as being concerned therein and approvers thereof. Thirdly. Because it hath a tendency to undo that continental harmony and friendship which yourselves by your late liberal and charitable donations hath lent a hand to establish; and the preservation of which, is of the utmost consequence to us all.

And here, without anger or resentment I bid you farewell. Sincerely wishing, that as men and Christians, ye may always fully and uninterruptedly *enjoy every civil and religious right; and be, in your turn, the means of securing it to others; but that the example which ye have unwisely set, of mingling religion with politics, may be disavowed and reprobated by every inhabitant of America."*

The brief chapter above is how Thomas Paine ended his original version of "Common Sense." The Epistle, or letter, was not listed on the cover, just as this missive is not, but those few words are why, when Paine died in 1809, only six people attended his funeral. This despite Paine having been one of the most popular and successful authors of his time,

Paine was the son of a Quaker father, but like Thomas Jefferson, and several others of the Founding Fathers, Paine had a real problem with organized religion, especially when organized religion tried to interject itself into politics.

At the time of the American Revolution many religious organizations were actively working to make themselves players in the political arena, but none were more overt in their efforts than the Quakers.

Paine's letter was an attempt to persuade the Quakers to stay out of the political upheaval surrounding the revolution, and to allow the secular community to direct the conflict and decide upon the laws that would govern the fledgling nation to come without religious interference.

Paine's Epistle is a difficult read for the modern mind, but reduced to its essence Paine is politely asking the Quakers to enjoy the religious and political freedoms that the revolution would surely ensure for all Americans, but to keep their noses, and their religion, out of politics.

The Quakers, and many other prominent religious leaders and organizations in the new America, did not accept Paine's polite reproach in the spirit that Paine had intended, and they vehemently condemned him for it for the rest of his life.

I too have a real problem with organized religion, and especially with the manner in which the far-right Christian and Fundamentalist Islamic communities are attempting to interject themselves into today's modern political arena.

I personally do not care in the least what any person's religious affiliations are, and I have never understood why people cannot worship as they choose, or not worship as they choose, and allow others to do the same. To my simple mind a person's faith, or lack thereof, neither qualifies nor disqualifies them for holding political office, nor does it validate or invalidate their arguments or opinions.

It is my fervent hope that these few words that I have penned will inspire others to work to change the political and socioeconomic mess that our great nation has become.

It is also my most sincere desire that all men and women, of all religious beliefs and persuasions, will leave their religious faith, or lack thereof, out of the very important debate that is surely to come.

-THE END-

P.S. Thank you, Thomas; both of you.

For the People

The poem on the following page is a gift from the Author to the People of the United States. It is reverently dedicated to the courageous men and women who fight and die to protect this great Republic, and to keep We the People free.

May We always recognize and honor their sacrifice; and let us pledge together that We will never again elect a government that will attempt to use our military as an extension of diplomacy, and thereby squander their precious lives like so many pieces on a geopolitical chessboard.

A Soldier's Soliloquy
By John Lollar

Moon!
Black sky punctuated by a cratered light
And stars!
Like inky satin dusted with points of white

Ghostly quiet
Blown asunder by cannonade
Awakens my senses
Even as they hasten to blunt and fade

Brothers scurry
And crave shelter from shot and shell
Scanning wildly
Searching for the hated jackals from hell

Distant screams
But I cannot tell from whom
For pain comes equally
To all of those that it marks for doom

Crescent and Cross
Both reap rose sorrow this night
And death's gatekeeper cares not
For what ensign the fallen did fight

Faces of my children
Through my muddled memory swarm
And the soft sweet arms
Where my love cradled me safe from harm

As the crimson stain
Across my heaving breast does grow
My torment wanes
But my slowing heart becomes heavy with woe

For only now
At the instant of life's curtain fall
Do I fully grasp
The folly of the clarion call

There can be no victor
In the battle that extinguishes my mind
Only we who move on
And the unknowing that are left behind